La Petite Ferme

COUNTRY CUISINE

Best Wishes & Bon Apetit!
Carol Dendy Young

La Petite Ferme

COUNTRY CUISINE

CAROL DENDY YOUNG

PHOTOGRAPHY BY PADDY HOWES

Struik Publishers
(a division of New Holland Publishing (South Africa) (Pty) Ltd)
Cornelis Struik House
80 McKenzie Street
Cape Town 8001
South Africa
New Holland Publishing is a member of the Johnnic Publishing Group

First published in 2002
2 4 6 8 10 9 7 5 3

Copyright © in published edition: Struik Publishers 2002
Copyright © in text: Carol Dendy Young (recipes) and Mark Dendy Young (Introduction) 2002
Copyright © in photographs: Carol Dendy Young 2002

All rights reserved. No part of this publication may be reproduced, stored in a retrieval system, or transmitted, in any form or by any means, electronic, mechanical, photocopying, recording or otherwise, without the prior written permission of the copyright owner/s.

Publishing manager: Linda de Villiers
Editor: Linda de Villiers
Designer: Petal Palmer
Design assistant: Sean Robertson
Photographer: Paddy Howes
Reproduction by Hirt & Carter Cape (Pty) Ltd
Printed and bound in Singapore by Craft Print

ISBN 1 86872 754 8

www.struik.co.za

Log on to our photographic website
www.imagesofafrica.co.za for an African experience.

Contents

Introduction 7

Soups 19

Starters & Salads 37

Main Courses 57

Side Dishes 87

Desserts 101

Miscellaneous 121

Index 127

Introduction

It's a golden summer's day: around you, as you drive through the Franschhoek valley, neatly laid out orchards and vineyards, backed by towering mountains, are food for the soul. But it's food of another kind you have in mind as you approach the village with its inviting sidewalk cafés and restaurants lining the main street. But why Franschhoek? Well, it's the rural setting, the location, less than an hour from Cape Town, and the climate. Cold, wet winters and hot, dry summers might not suit everyone, but wine grapes and deciduous fruit thrive in this climate, as do a host of vegetables and herbs. It does not take you long to appreciate why Franschhoek is considered the gourmet capital of the Cape.

It was the Mediterranean climate more than anything else that made it a home from home for the Huguenot settlers, three hundred years ago. Here they could live. Here they could grow grapes, make wine, grow the fruit they had plucked as children. Still nostalgic for the France they had left, however, they called their farms La Motte, Bourgogne, La Dauphine, La Provence.

Within a few years they found themselves speaking as much Dutch as their own French for they farmed side by side with the early Dutch settlers, who on a wider canvas outnumbered them. And it was one of these, Jean Jordaan, who in 1694 chose for his new home a corner of the valley with long, wide views and a high cliff at its back. Perhaps my father would have found in Jordaan a kindred spirit, for this is where he felt comfortable settling his family nearly three centuries later, in 1972. It was not the vast spread Jordaan possessed, but there was no doubt it was what he was looking for to grow top-quality fruit and vines. Perhaps it was because he would walk the perimeter in the same time as Jordaan would have ridden it, and was mindful that he was in the French Corner, that John called it La Petite Ferme, the small farm.

With its spectacular setting and outlook, close to the village and next to the road, it seemed the ideal setting for a small restaurant – the perfect spot for my mother, Carol, to sell fresh fruit, jams and preserves, as well as for serving teas and light lunches. The two of them, with input from grandmother Norah, designed a simple thatch-roofed building, which John and the farm staff built. Just before Christmas in 1984 they opened for business, with John and three 'waitresses' (and in those early days the inverted commas were called for at times) in front of house, and my mother and grandmother bent over stoves and mixing bowls, assisted by three willing but completely untrained helpers. Other than the three hotels in Franschhoek this was the third restaurant to open: it was a sign of the times that only twenty years ago many wise folk shook their heads, wondering whether the village could support that many.

Above: Hand-picked, plump and juicy plums.
Right: The many faces behind La Petite Ferme's success.

An idyllic spot for an after-lunch siesta.

My brothers and I were not surprised at our parents' decision. As youngsters we had always looked forward to mealtimes, knowing mum would serve us a fine spread of hearty country fare. We didn't think of it then, but the fact that it was nearly all home grown, often including the mutton from the small farm flock, fills us now with belated appreciation. My great-grandmother too, was an accomplished hands-on cook, turning fruit from her garden into delectable jams and preserves and using traditional methods to pickle vegetables. What remains with me now are the tantalising aromas of curry, cumin, cinnamon and nutmeg.

The signpost to a little patch of paradise.

In 1994, after many long hours of deliberation around the table, my new bride, Josephine, and I decided to buy the restaurant. I had been involved for a while and had loved it, and there was another string I wanted to add to the family bow. John Platter had managed to light a flame when I was eleven that still burned fiercely: I wanted to make wine. In my dad's characteristic style, it was within months of our making the decision to go into the wine business that the winery was built. The intention was mainly to satisfy the needs of the restaurant, and of those customers who found the wine to their liking.

Introduction

That was early in 1996, the same year that flames of a more literal kind were to burn fiercely. On May 22nd at 2.00 am, the roar of burning thatch and exploding gas bottles shattered the night quiet. The restaurant was on fire. We managed to save the winery but the restaurant was razed to the ground. It was a devastating blow, but there was little else to do but grit our teeth and throw ourselves into rebuilding. That we opened later that same year in our present iron-roofed premises can be attributed to teamwork and determination.

Clockwise from top left: Guest suites nestle on the slopes of the vineyards; Carol in the herb garden; Mark, Josephine and Timothy in the vineyards; father and son in the winery.

The luxury guest suites were built in 1997 as a logical step of vertical integration in the hospitality business. Josephine has a flare for decorating, as can be seen in the restaurant, and she applied her talent with characteristic enthusiasm to the new project.

La Petite Ferme remains what it has always been, a family affair. When you arrive the chances are that you will be warmly greeted by a member of the (extended) Dendy Young family. What you won't see, though, are the daily meetings we have over a cup of morning tea, when new additions to the menu are discussed, feedback from the previous day is reviewed, and comments on the wine and possible new directions in wine-making are examined. All views are welcomed and considered.

The wine that finds most favour with our guests is our Sauvignon Blanc, with its fresh taste and a bouquet that calls to mind green peppers and flint. But if it's something else you fancy there is a selection of twelve others, from the gorgeous, sparkling Belle Josephine, aptly named after my wife, to the more serious Shiraz.

Mark and Timothy – wine-maker in the wings.

'La Petite Ferme remains what it has always been, a family affair. When you arrive the chances are that you will be warmly greeted by a member of the Dendy Young family.'

Introduction

Mark emerging from the Maturation Cellar.

'The wine that finds most favour with our guests is our Sauvignon Blanc, with its fresh taste and a bouquet that calls to mind green peppers and flint.'

You should have a bottle of the Shiraz if you're on the terrace on a winter afternoon wondering whether you really do have to go home, when the distant snow-capped peaks are glowing warmly in the afternoon sunlight. The wine comes from the vines at the end of the lawn, now starkly brown. Imagine a time when they were – and will be again – a profusion of green, the fat black berries hiding shyly. And resolve to come back then.

Grapes are picked long before the summer sun gets onto them, in February, when they're swollen with sugary juice. Hotels are full then, too, for that's the peak of the annual northern hemisphere tourist migration to the south, so remember to book early if that's when you plan to spend a leisurely afternoon on our terrace.

Lunch on the terrace.

If we have been successful in our quest to provide a memorable gastronomic experience, I suppose it's because of our passion. Out of that passion grow hard work and loyalty: without it the downhill road is slippery and steep. And when you have been here you'll understand that it's a place that's easy to be passionate in, and passionate about.

With me it's the wine, from the time the grapes are tipped from the farm trailer right through the long, patient process to the moment when we anxiously taste the first fruits of our labour. Was everything done right, for the right length of time, at the right temperature, with the correct blending? My father is passionate about his vines, the drainage, the irrigation, the soil, the slope, the trellising, the sun, the rain, the wind. And the pruning. The winery is interconnected with the restaurant and the guest suites like the fibres of a cloth. Snip, snip, snip, hear the guests in the suites as they stretch that first stretch after a night of peace that no city knows: the men are pruning, or are they harvesting? Snip, snip. What shall we have for breakfast?

Whatever it is, it comes from a kitchen where dedication to excellence is the byword. And the enthusiasm – the only way my mother works – is infectious, irresistible. See it in the staff as they go about their work at La Petite Ferme.

And the loyalty is no different: our staff, many of whom have been with us since we opened, are loyal to us because they know we are loyal to them. They know we wouldn't ask them to do anything we wouldn't do; they work hard because they see us working hard. It would be wrong, though, to say the reason they enjoy it is because we do. No, the reason they find fulfilment is age-old: doing a job well is simply fulfilling. It's a visceral thing: they would look at you blankly if you spoke to them about commitment to excellence. It doesn't need words: it's just something you come to know. Doing it right feels good.

We like to think it's a blend of these ingredients that helps to create the most unforgettable lunch or stay at La Petite Ferme. This book is an invitation to share with us our passion for uncomplicated entertainment and country cuisine that cognoscenti come back for time and again and to experience a piece of heaven in your home.

Mark,

Mark Dendy Young

Chunky Mediterranean Soup

SERVES 6–8

*This soup should be chunky so take care not to over process.
It must be served very cold so add a few cubes of ice just before serving.
The olives are optional but add to the Mediterranean flavour.*

4 tomatoes, diced

1 red pepper, diced

1 green pepper, diced

1 large onion, diced

1 medium English cucumber, diced

1 litre (4 cups) Tomato Cocktail

15 ml (1 Tbsp) olive oil

125 ml (½ cup) balsamic vinegar

15 ml (1 Tbsp) brown sugar

salt and pepper to taste

approximately 250 ml (1 cup) water

125 ml (½ cup) chopped black olives (optional)

Combine all the ingredients and refrigerate for 2–3 hours but preferably overnight to allow the flavours to infuse.
This is a taste-and-test recipe so adjust the seasoning, adding more sugar if the tomatoes are tart.

WINE SUGGESTION: Chenin Blanc

Curried Apple Soup

SERVES 6

This has been one of our most popular soups. The unusual combination of curry and apple and the fact that the soup can be served either hot or cold, makes it a most useful addition to one's repertoire.

5 large fresh apples, peeled and sliced
1 large onion, sliced
4 medium potatoes, peeled and sliced
500 ml (2 cups) water
20 ml (4 tsp) curry powder
20 ml (4 tsp) oil
2.5 ml (½ tsp) mixed spice
2.5 ml (½ tsp) nutmeg
15 ml (1 Tbsp) chutney
15 ml (1 Tbsp) brown sugar
salt and pepper to taste
milk and cream

Simmer the apples, onion and potatoes in the water until soft, then blend to a smooth purée. To release the flavour, heat the curry powder (hot or mild) in the oil, then add to the purée together with the mixed spice, nutmeg, chutney, brown sugar, salt and pepper. To achieve the desired consistency, add milk and a little cream if desired.

WINE SUGGESTION: Muscat d'Alexandrie

Carrot and Ginger Soup

SERVES 6

Our version of Crème de Crecy is a taste sensation!

50 g butter
1 packet or 1 bunch carrots, scraped and sliced
2 leeks, sliced
1 large red pepper, chopped
1 litre (4 cups) chicken or vegetable stock
7.5 ml (1½ tsp) freshly grated root ginger
salt and pepper
20 ml (4 tsp) white sugar
125 ml (½ cup) cream
carrot rings, thinly sliced and grilled to garnish

Melt the butter and add the carrots, leeks and pepper. Stir well and allow to soften but not brown.
Add the stock, ginger, salt and pepper and sugar. Simmer for 20 minutes until the vegetables are soft.
Blend all together until smooth, then return to the saucepan and stir in the cream.
Reheat but do not allow to boil.
Serve hot or chilled, garnished with thinly sliced carrot rings crisped under the grill.

WINE SUGGESTION: Chenin Blanc

Spinach and Feta Soup

SERVES 6

This old favourite is often used in quiches but makes a tasty combination in soup.

2 large bunches spinach
2.5 ml (½ tsp) bicarbonate of soda
1 large onion, chopped
4 potatoes, peeled and chopped
salt and black pepper
225 g feta
milk and cream

De-vein the spinach and wash very well. Boil the spinach in fast boiling water to which the bicarbonate of soda has been added until the spinach is just cooked. Meanwhile, boil the onion and potatoes together until soft. Process the spinach, onion, potatoes, salt and pepper to taste and the feta to a smooth purée. Add milk and a little cream to bring the soup to the right consistency, then reheat gently or chill before serving.

WINE SUGGESTION: Sauvignon Blanc

Pear and Blue Cheese Soup

SERVES 6

When in season, we use pears grown on the farm and poach them until soft before puréeing. This soup, served either hot or chilled, has received many compliments.

1 large onion, chopped
butter
850 g tin pears, drained
1 wedge (125 g) blue cheese
40 ml (8 tsp) cornflour
500 ml (2 cups) milk
250 ml (1 cup) vegetable stock
salt and white pepper

Fry the onion in a little butter until soft.
Transfer to a food processor together with the pears and cheese and process until smooth. Blend the cornflour into the milk and gently bring the milk and stock to the boil, then remove immediately and add to the purée. Season to taste with salt and pepper. Serve either hot or chilled, garnished with a sliver of pear and a little grated blue cheese.

WINE SUGGESTION: Barrel-fermented Chardonnay

*For a lovely sweetish flavour,
add the juice from the tinned pears and adjust
the consistency of the soup if necessary.*

La Petite Ferme
COUNTRY CUISINE

Soups

Chilled Cucumber Soup

SERVES 4

There are many different ways of making this delicious summer soup but this is my version.

1 large English cucumber
50 g butter
1 medium onion, grated
50 g cake flour
500 ml (2 cups) hot milk
salt and white pepper to taste
150 ml (⅔ cup) plain yoghurt
cucumber and chopped fresh parsley to garnish

Grate the cucumber, then place it in a sieve over a bowl and allow it to drain to get rid of excess moisture. In the meantime, melt the butter, add the onion and allow to soften.
Stir in the flour over low heat. Remove saucepan from the heat and gradually stir in the hot milk until smooth and slightly thickened. Simmer gently for 5 minutes. Season with salt and white pepper.
Add the cucumber and stir to combine. Lastly stir in the yoghurt and chill very well before serving garnished with thinly sliced cucumber and a sprinkling of fresh parsley.

WINE SUGGESTION: Sauvignon Blanc

Mulligatawny Soup

SERVES 6

*This is an unusual soup not often seen in restaurants.
It originated in Colonial India and is lovely in winter with its warming curry flavour.*

2 potatoes, cubed

1 apple, grated

2 carrots, cut into rounds

15 ml (1 Tbsp) oil

20 ml (4 tsp) curry powder

15 ml (1 Tbsp) cake flour

1 litre (4 cups) beef, lamb or vegetable stock

15 ml (1 Tbsp) sultanas

15 ml (1 Tbsp) fruit chutney

salt and pepper to taste

sugar to taste

lemon juice to taste

Fry the potatoes, apple and carrots in the oil until lightly browned.
Stir in the curry powder and flour, then slowly add the stock.
Add the remaining ingredients and simmer for 45–60 minutes. Top up with additional stock or water so that the liquid does not diminish. Serve with a glass of sherry.

WINE SUGGESTION: Rhine Riesling (Dry)

Trout Bisque

SERVES 6–8

We use salmon trout in this soup, but any fish, such as tinned tuna or salmon, can be substituted. The success of this soup is the very rich stock made from smoked trout bones.

1 litre (4 cups) fish stock (page 123)
3 potatoes, peeled and chopped
2 carrots, scraped and chopped
2 leeks, sliced
2 sticks celery, chopped
500 g salmon trout, flaked
15 ml (1 Tbsp) tomato paste
500 ml (2 cups) milk
125 ml (½ cup) cream or plain yoghurt
salt and white pepper to taste
cream to garnish

Heat the stock and add the potatoes, carrots, leeks and celery. Simmer for 45–60 minutes until the vegetables are soft. Add the fish and tomato paste, then blend until smooth. Add the milk and cream, return to the saucepan and reheat gently. Do not allow to boil as it may curdle. Adjust the consistency by adding either more milk or cornflour mixed with a little water to form a smooth paste. Season to taste.
Serve piping hot and garnished with a swirl of cream.

WINE SUGGESTION: Blanc Fumé

La Petite Ferme
COUNTRY CUISINE

Potato and Spring Onion Soup

SERVES 6–8

Potatoes and onions have always combined well to make a creamy soup full of flavour.
Spring onions add interest and colour but I also add an onion for extra flavour and texture.

4–6 large potatoes, peeled and chopped
1 large onion, chopped
1 bunch spring onions, including some of the green tops, chopped
1 litre (4 cups) milk
125 ml (½ cup) cream
salt and pepper to taste
cream or plain yoghurt and snipped chives to garnish

Simmer the potatoes, onions and spring onions in enough water to cover until the vegetables are soft.
Blend until smooth, then add the milk, cream and salt and pepper.
Add more milk if a thinner consistency is required, or thicken with cornflour mixed with water
to form a smooth paste. Reheat gently but do not boil.
Serve the soup in warmed bowls and garnish with a swirl of cream or yoghurt and a sprinkling of chives.

WINE SUGGESTION: Semillon

Split Pea and Eisbein Soup

SERVES 6–8

1 large onion, chopped

1 smoked Eisbein knuckle

1x 500 g packet split peas, soaked overnight in water to cover

salt and black pepper to taste

5 ml (1 tsp) dry mustard

bread croûtons to garnish

Place the onion and Eisbein in a saucepan with enough water to cover and bring to the boil.
Reduce heat and simmer until the meat is soft and falls off the bone.
Keep topping up the water if the level gets too low. Remove the meat and chop roughly.
Reserve the cooking liquid, adding enough water to make up 1.5 litres (6 cups).
Cook the peas until soft in enough water to cover. Drain. Blend the peas with the reserved stock.
Return the liquid to the saucepan, add salt and pepper, the mustard and meat and reheat gently until piping hot.
Garnish with croûtons and serve.

WINE SUGGESTION: Shiraz

Fish Pot

SERVES 6–8

This recipe is for fish lovers and any fish or seafood can be added. It can be as extravagant or as thrifty as you choose.

30 ml (2 Tbsp) olive oil
4 cloves garlic, crushed
2 onions, chopped
125 ml (½ cup) dry white wine
60 ml (¼ cup) tomato paste
2 x 410 g tins whole tomatoes, chopped
2 bay leaves
10 ml (2 tsp) sugar
250 ml (1 cup) water
500 ml (2 cups) fish stock
500 g fish, chopped
250 g calamari tubes
250 g mussel meat
500 g uncooked shelled prawns or marinara mixed seafood

Heat the oil in a large pot and sauté the garlic and onions until soft.
Add the wine, tomato paste, tomatoes, bay leaves, sugar and water and simmer for 10 minutes.
Add the cleaned and prepared seafood and bring to the boil.
Cover, reduce the heat and simmer on low heat for 5 minutes. Serve immediately with a crusty French loaf.

WINE SUGGESTION: Sauvignon Blanc

Rich Onion and Herb Soup

SERVES 6

This winter soup with its attractive bubbling cheese topping is hearty and warming.

6 large onions
125 ml (½ cup) olive oil
125 ml (½ cup) finely chopped fresh or 20 ml (4 tsp) dried mixed herbs
15 ml (1 Tbsp) cake flour
1 litre (4 cups) hot beef, chicken or vegetable stock
5 ml (1 tsp) coarse black pepper
5 ml (1 tsp) salt
125 ml (½ cup) balsamic vinegar
20 ml (4 tsp) brown sugar
125 ml (½ cup) red wine
3 slices bread, halved
gruyère cheese, grated
finely chopped fresh herbs to garnish

Slice the onions into thick rings and brown lightly in the olive oil.
Stir in the herbs and flour, then add the stock and simmer for a few minutes.
Add the remaining ingredients, except the bread, cheese and herb garnishing, and simmer for 10 minutes.
In the meantime, toast the bread, top with grated cheese and grill until bubbling.
Ladle the soup into warm bowls, top with the grilled cheese toasts and sprinkle with chopped herbs.
Serve immediately.

WINE SUGGESTION: Wooded Chenin Blanc

Starters & Salads

Chicken Liver Pâté

SERVES 8

This pâté is delicious served on crisp slices of Melba toast, French bread or savoury biscuits.

125 g butter
500 g chicken livers, cleaned
1 medium onion
7.5 ml (1½ tsp) salt
5 ml (1 tsp) coarse black pepper
10 ml (2 tsp) prepared English mustard
180 ml (¾ cup) cream
15 ml (1 Tbsp) brandy

Melt the butter in a frying pan and sauté the livers and onion for about 5 minutes until the onion is soft and the livers firm. Season with salt and pepper. Stir in the mustard.
Blend until smooth, then add the cream and brandy.
Pour into eight 125 ml (½ cup) ramekins and refrigerate until set.

WINE SUGGESTION: Noble Late Harvest

An easy way of making Melba toast is to toast sliced 3-day-old white bread in the toaster. Split the slices with a sharp knife and toast the untoasted side under the grill.

Salmon Trout Mousse

SERVES 8

*We had removed this starter from the menu only to bring it back by popular demand.
We thought you might like to have the recipe.*

450 g salmon trout, flaked or
2x 200 g tins tuna, drained
5 ml (1 tsp) finely chopped fennel or dill
5 ml (1 tsp) finely chopped spring onion
salt and pepper to taste
30 ml (2 Tbsp) gelatine
45 ml (3 Tbsp) water
15 ml (1 Tbsp) mayonnaise
15 ml (1 Tbsp) tomato paste
250 ml (1 cup) fresh cream, whipped
caviar to garnish

Fennel Yoghurt Sauce
60 ml (¼ cup) firmly packed finely chopped fennel or dill
10 ml (2 tsp) lemon juice
2.5 ml (½ tsp) salt
2.5 ml (½ tsp) white pepper
250 ml (1 cup) plain yoghurt

Blend the fish, fennel, spring onion and salt and pepper. In a small bowl, sprinkle the gelatine over the water. When the water has been absorbed, place the bowl in hot water over low heat and stir until gelatine has dissolved. Stir the gelatine, mayonnaise and tomato paste into the fish mixture, then fold in the whipped cream.
Spoon into eight 125 ml (½ cup) greased moulds or cups and refrigerate until firm.
Make the yoghurt sauce by mixing all the ingredients together, then refrigerate until ready to serve. Unmould the mousse and serve with the yoghurt sauce and a sprinkling of caviar or straviar for that extra-special occasion.

WINE SUGGESTION: Blanc Fumé

Mushrooms en Croûte

SERVES 4

Any mushrooms can be used but the large brown ones are the most flavoursome and attractive.

butter and a little olive oil
500 g brown mushrooms, thickly sliced
3 spring onions, chopped
15 ml (1 Tbsp) chopped fresh or 2.5 ml (½ tsp) dried mixed herbs
salt and coarse black pepper
125 ml (½ cup) cream
4 slices buttered toast to serve
snipped chives or chopped parsley to garnish

Heat the butter and oil and add mushrooms, onions, herbs, salt and pepper.
Cook quickly over a high heat, shaking the pan now and then, until brown and interesting.
Mushrooms must still be firm. Stir in the cream.
Use a large cookie cutter to cut out rounds of buttered toast.
Spoon the mushrooms onto the buttered toast rounds and sprinkle with chives or parsley.

WINE SUGGESTION: Chenin Blanc

Crumbed Mussels

SERVES 6

We can buy delicious plump black mussels from the West Coast and have prepared them in many different ways. These crumbed ones are easy and so delicious.

750 ml (3 cups) soft white breadcrumbs
125 g melted butter
20 ml (4 tsp) chopped fresh parsley
100 g blue cheese, crumbled
10 ml (2 tsp) crushed garlic
black mussels (allow 6 per person)

Mix the breadcrumbs, butter, parsley, blue cheese and garlic into a crumbly mixture.
Spoon the mixture over the mussels and brown under the grill.
Serve on a patch of rice, pasta or simply on their own with a squeeze of lemon juice.

WINE SUGGESTION: Wooded Chardonnay

Starters & Salads

Chicken and Almond Salad

SERVES 4

Josephine, my daughter-in-law, loves this starter, which we served at her 21st birthday. The marinating takes a little extra time but it is really worth the effort.

6 chicken breasts
250 ml (1 cup) cake flour
100 g flaked almonds
about 250 ml (1 cup) oil for frying
salad greens
snipped chives to garnish

Marinade
180 ml (¾ cup) soya sauce
125 ml (½ cup) medium cream sherry
5 ml (1 tsp) finely grated root ginger
2.5 ml (½ tsp) finely grated garlic

Dressing
125 ml (½ cup) vinegar
60 ml (¼ cup) sugar
20 ml (4 tsp) soya sauce
125 ml (½ cup) oil
2.5 ml (½ tsp) white pepper

First mix together all the marinade ingredients. Flatten the chicken breasts with a meat mallet and place in a bowl in a single layer. Pour marinade over chicken and refrigerate overnight. Remove meat from marinade and allow to drain. Mix the flour and almonds and coat the chicken pieces well. Fry quickly in hot oil, then drain on kitchen paper. Slice the chicken into strips and arrange over salad greens. Garnish with chives. Mix together the dressing ingredients and sprinkle over the salad just before serving.

WINE SUGGESTION: Unwooded Chardonnay

Hot Grain Salad

SERVES 4 AS A STARTER OR 2 AS A MAIN MEAL

*This salad is served hot which makes it unusual and quite useful for colder days.
Any grain or pulse can be used but I prefer the combination of rice, wild rice, lentils and cracked wheat or barley.*

125 ml (½ cup) white or brown rice
125 ml (½ cup) wild rice
125 ml (½ cup) brown lentils
125 ml (½ cup) cracked wheat or barley
water
salt to taste
4 spring onions, finely chopped
15 ml (1 Tbsp) chopped fresh mint
15 ml (1 Tbsp) chopped fresh parsley
75 ml (5 Tbsp) olive oil
juice of 1 lemon
coarse black pepper
sesame seeds and parsley to garnish

Rinse both rices, lentils and cracked wheat or barley under running water.

Place the white or brown rice and barley in a saucepan and add 1.5 litres (6 cups) water and 5 ml (1 tsp) salt and bring to the boil. Place the lentils and wild rice in another saucepan and add 1.5 litres (6 cups) water and 5 ml (1 tsp) salt and bring to the boil. Reduce heat and simmer until cooked.

Pour the grains into a colander and allow to drain. Mix the grains with the spring onions, mint, parsley, oil, lemon juice and pepper, then serve warm sprinkled with sesame seeds and parsley.

WINE SUGGESTION: Light White Blend

Chickpeas, beans or couscous all make wonderful options.

Guacamole with Spicy Chilli Salsa

SERVES 6–8

The spicy chilli sauce is the perfect accompaniment to this Mexican favourite.

3 ripe avocados, mashed
20 ml (4 tsp) chopped onion
10 ml (2 tsp) lemon juice
5 ml (1 tsp) Worcester sauce
125 ml (½ cup) mayonnaise
2.5 ml (½ tsp) salt
2.5 ml (½ tsp) white pepper
125 ml (½ cup) cream
125 ml (½ cup) milk
20 ml (4 tsp) gelatine
45 ml (3 Tbsp) water
fresh coriander to garnish
nacho chips to serve

Salsa

3 tomatoes, skinned and finely chopped
½ red chilli, seeded and finely chopped
½ small onion, finely chopped
juice of 1 lime or 20 ml (4 tsp) lime juice
30 ml (2 Tbsp) chopped coriander
salt and black pepper to taste

Place the avocado, onion, lemon juice, Worcester sauce, mayonnaise, salt and pepper in a food processor and process until smooth.
Blend in the cream and milk.
Sprinkle the gelatine over the water in a small bowl and when all the water has been absorbed, place the bowl in hot water over low heat and stir to dissolve.
Blend the gelatine into the avocado mixture and pour into 125 ml (½ cup) moulds or cups or a bowl.
Refrigerate until set.
Make the salsa by combining all the ingredients.
Unmould the avocado onto serving plates
(or spoon out if you have used a bowl)
and place a spoonful of salsa alongside.
Garnish with fresh coriander and serve
with a few nacho chips to scoop up the
avo and salsa.

WINE SUGGESTION: Blanc de Noir

Smoked Salmon and Blinis

SERVES 6–8/MAKES 20 MEDIUM-SIZE BLINIS

The blinis, which look so attractive with the green of the chopped chives folded into the mixture, add substance to this light dish.

salad greens
500 g smoked salmon slices

Chive Sauce
125 ml (½ cup) yoghurt
125 ml (½ cup) mayonnaise
125 ml (½ cup) cream
125 ml (½ cup) firmly packed snipped chives

Blinis
2 eggs, separated
125 ml (½ cup) water
125 ml (½ cup) milk
125 ml (½ cup) plain yoghurt
500 ml (2 cups) self-raising flour
5 ml (1 tsp) baking powder
2.5 ml (½ tsp) salt
7.5 ml (1½ tsp) coarse black pepper
1 bunch spring onions (including some of the green part) or chives, finely chopped

For the sauce, mix all the ingredients together and set aside.
To make the blinis, whisk the egg whites until stiff. Mix all the remaining ingredients together, then gently fold in the egg whites – do not overmix.
Drop teaspoonsful on to a warm, oiled frying pan. When bubbles appear on the surface of each blini, turn them over and cook the other side.
Remove and keep warm. Continue making blinis until all the mixture has been used up.
For each serving, arrange 3 blinis on a plate, add fresh crisp salad greens to one side.
Top with curled salmon slices and drizzle with the Chive sauce.

WINE SUGGESTION: Sparkling Wine

Starters & Salads

Trout Terrine

MAKES 10–12 SLICES

We have an abundance of trout in Franschhoek, and as it seems to be available throughout the country I have included this rather glamorous starter.

smoked salmon slices
250 g flaked smoked salmon
500 g salmon trout offcuts
1 x 170 g tin tuna
100 g butter, melted
15 ml (1 Tbsp) finely chopped dill
15 ml (1 Tbsp) white wine
15 ml (1 Tbsp) lemon juice
150 ml (⅗ cup) mayonnaise

22.5 ml (4½ tsp) gelatine dissolved in a little warm water
salt and coarse black pepper
200 ml (⅘ cup) whipped cream

Dill Sauce

20 ml (4 tsp) chopped dill
125 ml (½ cup) plain yoghurt
15 ml (1 Tbsp) cream
lemon juice to taste

Line a narrow bread tin with strips of smoked salmon, leaving enough to fold over at the end.
Mix fish, butter, dill, wine, lemon juice, mayonnaise, gelatine, salt and pepper together.
Stir gently so as to maintain a texture in the fish. Finally fold in the whipped cream.
Spoon into the lined tin, fold over the salmon ends to cover the top, and place in the refrigerator overnight until firm.
Slice with a very sharp knife and serve with a spoonful of dill sauce.
To make the dill sauce, mix all the ingredients together.

WINE SUGGESTION: **Chardonnay**

Malay Pickled Fish

SERVES 6–8

This is another La Petite Ferme favourite, made by Mary who makes it with great love and care, choosing her own spices and fish.

800 g–1 kg large fish fillets (I use hake), cut into portions
15 ml (1 Tbsp) salt
15 ml (1 Tbsp) dried mixed herbs
100 g butter
3 onions, sliced
1 green pepper, sliced
1 red pepper, sliced
125 ml (½ cup) raisins

Sauce
125 ml (½ cup) oil
125 ml (½ cup) chutney
25 ml (5 tsp) mild curry powder
10 ml (2 tsp) salt
250 ml (1 cup) white vinegar
250 ml (1 cup) brown vinegar
500 ml (2 cups) water
15 ml (1 Tbsp) whole black peppercorns
about 15 ml (1 Tbsp) cornflour

Use any large fish fillets such as hake and cut into portions. Place on a baking tray, sprinkle with salt and a few herbs and dot with butter. Cover with foil and bake at 180 °C for 30 minutes. Take care not to overcook the fish. Make the sauce by combining all the ingredients together, except the cornflour. Bring to the boil, then simmer for 4–5 minutes. Blend the cornflour with a little water and stir into the sauce until thickened.
In a Pyrex baking dish, alternate layers of fish, onion, red and green pepper and raisins.
Pour over the sauce, ensuring all the fish is covered, cover with the lid or clingwrap and refrigerate for at least 12 hours before using. The flavour improves with time and the dish can be made a week in advance.
Serve with a fresh salad on a hot summer's day.

WINE SUGGESTION: Muscat d'Alexandrie

Starters & Salads

Smoked Kudu Salad with Blue Cheese Dressing

SERVES 2 AS A STARTER

If you like biltong, you will enjoy this gamey salad.

1 medium red pepper
1 medium yellow pepper
1 medium green pepper
1 small packet mixed salad greens
3 spring onions, chopped
150 g sliced smoked kudu

Dressing
30 g blue cheese
20 ml (4 tsp) sour cream or plain yoghurt
125 ml (½ cup) cream
15 ml (1 Tbsp) lemon juice

Grill the peppers skin-side up until the skin blackens and blisters.
Peel away the skin and cut the peppers into strips.
Combine the salad greens, spring onions and peppers and arrange kudu slices on top.
Drizzle with blue cheese dressing.
To make the dressing, combine all the ingredients together.

WINE SUGGESTION: Pinotage (medium bodied)

Spinach and Bacon Salad

MAKES 4 SMALL SALADS OR 1 TABLE SALAD

The secret of this salad is succulent young spinach leaves well dressed and beautifully presented.

30 ml (2 Tbsp) oil
1 onion, finely chopped
1x 250 g packet chopped bacon pieces
500 g baby spinach leaves
salt and coarse black pepper
cherry tomatoes
spring onions to garnish

Heat the oil in a large saucepan, and sauté the onion and bacon until lightly browned.
Remove from heat and add spinach leaves, stirring to coat leaves with oil.
Season with salt and pepper and arrange cherry tomatoes on top. Shred the green part of the spring onion and garnish the salad. Serve warm.

WINE SUGGESTION: Pinot Noir

Starters & Salads

Main Courses

Fish Fillets with Two Toppings

SERVES 6

Use either of these toppings on any favourite fish. They both add interest and are full of flavour.

6 thick fish steaks such as kingklip,
cob or Cape salmon
melted butter
lemon juice

Mustard Topping
100 g butter
15 ml (1 Tbsp) prepared mild mustard
15 ml (1 Tbsp) mustard seeds
juice of ½ lemon

Mediterranean Topping with Sun-dried Tomatoes
100 g sun-dried tomatoes, cut into pieces
30 whole cloves garlic
125 ml (½ cup) rosemary sprigs
180 ml (¾ cup) olive oil
2.5 ml (½ tsp) salt

Brush the fish with melted butter, squeeze over the lemon juice and grill under a preheated grill for 5–7 minutes on either side, depending on the thickness, until just done.
For the mustard topping, melt the butter, stir in the other ingredients and spoon over the fish steaks. Place under the heated grill and allow the top to brown.
For the Mediterranean topping, place all the ingredients into a small bowl and allow to marinate overnight. Spoon the mixture onto the top of the precooked fish steaks and place under the grill for about 3 minutes, until soft and brown.

WINE SUGGESTION: Wooded Chardonnay

Salmon Trout Parcels

SERVES 6

Salmon trout fillets are obtainable from Woolworths.

butter
1 leek, cut into rings
250 g button mushrooms, sliced
125 ml (½ cup) plain yoghurt
salt and coarse black pepper to taste
puff pastry
6 salmon trout fillets
1 egg yolk. beaten

Hollandaise Sauce
4 egg yolks
45 ml (3 Tbsp) hot water
juice of 1 lemon
125 ml (½ cup) melted butter
20 ml (4 tsp) chopped dill or fennel

Melt the butter and fry the leek lightly. When soft, add the mushrooms and cook until soft. Stir in the yoghurt and season with salt and pepper. Cool. Cut two rectangles of puff pastry to the size of each fillet. Place a fillet on one rectangle and top with the leek and mushroom mixture. Cover with the second pastry rectangle and refrigerate until firm. Paint with egg yolk and cut slits in pastry. Bake in a very hot oven at 200 °C for 15–20 minutes. Serve with a fresh salad and hollandaise sauce. To make the hollandaise sauce, beat the egg yolks and hot water over very low heat or in a double boiler. Continue beating while adding the lemon juice, butter and dill or fennel until the sauce is slightly thickened.

WINE SUGGESTION: **Sparkling Wine (Dry)**

La Petite Ferme
COUNTRY CUISINE

Main Courses

La Petite Ferme
COUNTRY CUISINE
60

Calamari Mediterranean Style

SERVES 6

In this Portuguese recipe any calamari can be used but we use the baby calamari tubes and tentacles. It is important to marinate the calamari and to cook it very quickly to avoid toughening. I have had some success in tenderising the large tubes by boiling them in a little water to which bicarb has been added and then marinating. This is not ideal and does tend to give the calamari a rather floury texture.

1 kg calamari
3 cloves garlic, chopped
15 ml (1 Tbsp) tomato paste
5 ml (1 tsp) dried mixed herbs
125 ml (½ cup) olive oil
15 ml (1 Tbsp) lemon juice

Place the calamari into a container with a lid and stir in the remaining ingredients.
Seal and refrigerate for at least a day, stirring occasionally.
Spoon the calamari into a hot pan or onto a grill plate and keep turning the calamari until cooked through – it only takes 3–4 minutes.
Serve on fluffy white rice with a fresh Mediterranean salad.

WINE SUGGESTION: **Pinotage**

Stuffed Baby Chickens

SERVES 6

Baby chickens are obtainable from Woolworths; they must be small and you will need one per person. Make sure the chickens are cleaned inside and out by washing them in water to which a little salt and vinegar have been added.

6 baby chickens

Stuffing
6 slices wholewheat bread, crumbed
2 onions, chopped
125 ml (½ cup) chopped fresh herbs (thyme and rosemary)
125 ml (½ cup) chopped pecan nuts
20 ml (4 tsp) soya sauce
125 ml (½ cup) olive oil

Sauce
375 ml (1½ cups) reserved chicken juices
20 ml (4 tsp) honey
20 ml (4 tsp) lemon juice
20 ml (4 tsp) soya sauce
salt and pepper
cornflour to thicken

Mix all the stuffing ingredients together and fill each chicken cavity. Tie the legs together with string to keep the stuffing in place.

Place in a roasting pan and cover with foil. Roast at 180 °C for 45 minutes, then remove the foil and brown for 15 minutes. Make sure the chickens are cooked through. Remove and keep warm. Reserve the cooking juices.

To make the sauce, combine all the ingredients, except the cornflour, and bring to the boil.
Mix cornflour with a little cold water and add to liquid, stirring until thickened slightly, then serve with the chickens.

WINE SUGGESTION: Unwooded Chardonnay

Chicken Roulade with Light Curry Sauce

SERVES 6

1 chicken or 6 chicken breasts,
deboned and flattened
spinach leaves, blanched in boiling water

Filling
6 chicken breasts, minced or finely chopped
1 red pepper, finely chopped
4 spring onions, finely chopped
salt and coarse black pepper

Curry Sauce
15 ml (1 Tbsp) oil
15 ml (1 Tbsp) chopped onion
20 ml (4 tsp) curry powder
15 ml (1 Tbsp) tomato purée
125 ml (½ cup) red wine
180 ml (¾ cup) water
1 bay leaf
pinch sugar
salt and pepper
2 thin slices lemon
2.5 ml (½ tsp) smooth apricot jam
250 ml (1 cup) mayonnaise
125 ml (½ cup) cream

Line the whole, deboned chicken or flattened chicken breasts with the spinach.
Mix all the ingredients together for the filling, then spread the mixture thickly on the chicken, roll up neatly and tie with string.
Place the chicken on a greased baking tray and bake at 160 °C until cooked through, about 1 hour for the whole chicken or 20–30 minutes for the chicken breasts. Allow to cool and firm up.
To make the sauce, heat the oil and sauté the onion until soft. Stir in the curry powder, then add the tomato purée, wine, water, bayleaf, sugar, salt and pepper, lemon and jam. Simmer for a few minutes, then strain. Stir in the mayonnaise and cream.
To serve, remove the string from the chicken, then cut into slices using a sharp knife. Arrange 2–3 slices on each plate, overlapping, to form an attractive arrangement, then pour over some of the sauce. Serve hot with vegetables or cold with salads.

WINE SUGGESTION: Rhine Riesling

La Petite Ferme
COUNTRY CUISINE
66

Thai Chilli Chicken Breasts

SERVES 6

6 chicken breast fillets
cake flour
salt and pepper
oil for frying

Chilli Sauce
1 small red pepper
1 small green pepper
5 ml (1 tsp) grated fresh root ginger
3 spring onions, chopped
30 ml (2 Tbsp) sweet chilli sauce

Flatten the chicken breasts with a meat mallet. Dust with seasoned flour and fry quickly in heated oil.
Drain on a paper towel, then slice into strips.
There are lots of very good sweet chilli sauces but I would like to suggest that you add red and green pepper, ginger and spring onions. Cut the peppers into thin strips, fry quickly with the ginger and spring onions.
Stir in the sweet chilli sauce and thicken with cornflour if necessary.
Spoon the sauce over the chicken strips and serve with fragrant Thai rice and a crisp green salad.

WINE SUGGESTION: Chenin Blanc

Panfried Duck and Plum Sauce

SERVES 6

We try to use the fruit and vegetables from the farm and once again have the opportunity to use our plums to make plum sauce. An easy alternative to fresh plums is plum jam.

6 duck breasts
oil to cover pan bottom for shallow frying
salt for each breast

Plum Sauce
180 ml (¾ cup) water
salt and pepper
30 ml (2 Tbsp) plum jam or 6 fresh plums
20 ml (4 tsp) soya sauce

Cut several slits across each breast through the skin and fat as this will help to release the fat and crisp the skin.
Heat the oil in the pan and when nice and hot place the duck breasts, skin side down.
Cook over medium heat for 5–8 minutes. Remove breasts, season with salt and keep warm.
To make the plum sauce, add the water to the pan juices and bring to the boil. Add salt and pepper to taste.
Add the plum jam and soya sauce and allow to reduce until syrupy.
If using fresh plums, halve them and remove the pip.
Slice, then place in a small saucepan with 60 ml (4 Tbsp) sugar and 200 ml (⅘ cup) water and simmer gently until soft.
Cool, then pass through a sieve and use instead of the jam.
Slice the breasts and arrange on warm plates. Spoon over the sauce. The combination of sweet and sour is delicious.

WINE SUGGESTION: Merlot

Main Courses

Pork Medallions and Prunes

SERVES 6

3 pork fillets
butter
flour
salt and pepper

Prune Sauce

15 ml (1 Tbsp) chopped onions
2.5 ml (½ tsp) crushed garlic
20 ml (4 tsp) butter
250 g prunes, stoned and cut into pieces
250 ml (1 cup) meat stock
15 ml (1 Tbsp) sherry
5 ml (1 tsp) brown sugar
5 ml (1 tsp) balsamic vinegar
salt and coarse black pepper to taste

Remove thin membrane and sinew on one side of each pork fillet. Heat a large frying pan or griddle and melt a knob of butter. Dust the fillets with seasoned flour and quickly brown on all sides. Keep turning until cooked through, then remove and set aside. In a clean saucepan, fry the onions and garlic in the butter until nicely browned, then add the prune pieces and the remaining ingredients and simmer until reduced and slightly thickened. To serve, slice the pork into medallions and spoon over the sauce.

WINE SUGGESTION: Shiraz

Bobotie

SERVES 4

*I had to include the recipe for this traditional dish as it is so popular.
Bobotie can be served as a simple supper or as the main course of a traditional dinner.*

60 g butter or margarine
1 large onion, chopped
15 ml (1 Tbsp) curry powder
2 slices white bread, crusts removed
125 ml (½ cup) milk
500 g minced lamb or beef (lean)
125 ml (½ cup) seedless raisins
45 ml (3 Tbsp) lemon juice
30 ml (2 Tbsp) fruit chutney
5 ml (1 tsp) salt
black pepper
1 egg
lemon leaves or bay leaves

Melt the butter, add the onion and sauté until soft. Stir in the curry powder.
Soak bread in the milk. Squeeze out and reserve the milk and add the bread to the onion together with the mince, raisins, lemon juice, chutney, salt and pepper. Cook for 5 minutes, stirring, then transfer to a shallow casserole dish.
In a small bowl, beat the reserved milk with the egg and pour over the mince. Bake at 160 °C for 30 minutes.
Remove from the oven and insert a few rolled lemon leaves or bay leaves to garnish.

WINE SUGGESTION: Gewürztraminer

Greek Lamb and Minted Yoghurt

SERVES 6

1 leg of lamb
olive oil
lemon juice
whole garlic cloves
sprigs of fresh rosemary
coarse salt

Minted Yoghurt
250 ml (1 cup) Bulgarian yoghurt
coarse black pepper
125 ml (½ cup) chopped fresh mint

Rub the lamb with olive oil and lemon juice. Pierce the meat and fill the slits with garlic and sprigs of rosemary.
Sprinkle with coarse salt and place in an oven bag in a roasting pan.
Roast at 100 °C overnight or for at least 12 hours.
The meat should fall off the bone and be succulent and tender.
Combine all the ingredients for the minted yoghurt.
Serve the lamb with a dollop of yoghurt sauce and a sprinkling of chopped mint with browned
aubergine slices and couscous.

WINE SUGGESTION: Cabernet Sauvignon / Merlot

Medallions of Beef and Oyster Mushrooms

SERVES 6

Fillet needs no introduction, but oyster mushrooms are a new variation to mushroom sauce.

6 x 200 g pieces of fillet steak
butter for frying

Oyster Mushroom Sauce

60 g butter
500 g oyster mushrooms
1 clove garlic, crushed
30 ml (2 Tbsp) white wine
125 ml (½ cup) water
125 ml (½ cup) cream

Pan-fry or grill the steaks in the butter to your liking. Set aside and keep warm.
Melt the butter, add the mushrooms and garlic, and sauté for 3 minutes.
Remove the mushrooms and set aside.
Add the wine, water and cream and simmer for 5 minutes until the sauce thickens slightly.
Add the mushrooms, heat through, then spoon on top of the steak medallions and serve immediately.

WINE SUGGESTION: Cabernet Franc

Liver and Bacon

SERVES 6

This has become an absolute favourite on our winter menu. It is very easy and very tasty.

1 kg lamb's liver, cleaned and thickly sliced
35 ml (7 tsp) cake flour
5 ml (1 tsp) dried mixed herbs
salt and pepper
butter or oil for frying
2 large onions, cut into rings
250 g bacon

Dust the liver with 15 ml (1 Tbsp) seasoned flour. The best way to do this is to place the flour, herbs and salt and pepper in a plastic bag. Add the liver and give the bag a good shake.
Heat the butter or oil and fry the liver until cooked to your preference.
Some like liver well done, others prefer it 'pink'. Remove from the pan and keep warm.
Make up a little gravy by browning the remaining flour in the pan in which the liver was cooked, then stir in some water and season with salt and pepper.
In another pan, fry the onions with the bacon until the onion is brown and the bacon crisp.
Arrange liver slices on a plate, pour over a little gravy to moisten, then top with bacon and onions.
Serve with fluffy mashed potatoes and a wedge of grilled tomato.

WINE SUGGESTION: Shiraz

Venison with Red Wine Sauce

SERVES 6

Venison is obtainable at many butcheries.
We use springbok loin or super cut, which usually comes vacuum sealed.

1 kg springbok loin or super cut

Marinade
15 ml (1 Tbsp) tomato paste
250 ml (1 cup) olive oil
15 ml (1 Tbsp) brown sugar
2 cloves garlic, chopped
5 ml (1 tsp) whole black peppercorns
5 ml (1 tsp) green peppercorns
500 ml (2 cups) red wine
5 ml (1 tsp) chopped fresh rosemary

Red Wine Sauce
15 ml (1 Tbsp) chopped onion
1 clove garlic, crushed
15 ml (1 Tbsp) butter
10 ml (2 tsp) cake flour
salt and coarse black pepper to taste
250 ml (1 cup) red wine
pinch brown sugar

Cut the meat into fillet-shaped, single portions and place in a ceramic bowl with a lid.
Mix all the marinade ingredients together and pour over the meat. Cover and refrigerate for at least 24 hours but preferably for three days.
Pan-fry or grill the meat to choice (rare, medium or well done). Venison is best served rare but there are those who prefer it more well done.
To make the red wine sauce, sauté the onion and garlic in the butter until brown.
Stir in the flour and salt and pepper.
Pour in the wine and bring to a boil.
Remove from the heat, strain, then return the sauce to the pan. If too thin, boil until the correct consistency is reached – it should be velvety smooth.
Stir in the sugar to bring out the flavour.
To serve, slice the meat into portions and spoon over the red wine sauce.

WINE SUGGESTION: Shiraz

Main Courses

Kudu Casserole

SERVES 8

*Nothing is more welcoming on a cold winter's day than a hearty casserole.
This recipe is best made a day or two before and deep-freezes very well.*

1.5 kg kudu or any other venison or beef
120 g butter
30 ml (2 Tbsp) brandy
250 g button mushrooms
200 g baby onions
500 ml (2 cups) dry red wine
250 ml (1 cup) port
250 ml (1 cup) water
125 ml (½ cup) tomato purée
2 bay leaves
30 ml (2 Tbsp) cornflour

Cut the meat into large cubes. Heat half the butter in a large pan and brown the meat well.
Add the brandy and flame.
Remove the meat and set aside.
Add the remaining butter and brown the whole mushrooms and baby onions.
Remove mushrooms and onions and set aside.
Return the meat to the pan and add the wine, port, water, tomato purée and bay leaves and simmer for 1 hour, covered, until the meat is tender.
Add the mushrooms and onions and simmer, uncovered, for another 30 minutes.
Mix cornflour with a little water to form a paste and stir into the stew to thicken the gravy.
Serve with Rosemary Mash (page 92) and green vegetables.

WINE SUGGESTION: **Cabernet Sauvignon / Merlot**

Vegetarian Parcel

SERVES 6

This is light and tasty — a popular vegetarian option.

phyllo pastry sheets
melted butter

Filling
50 ml (10 tsp) olive oil
300 g mushrooms, chopped
2 leeks, finely chopped
1 small onion, finely chopped
500 g cooked spinach, chopped
250 g chunky cottage cheese
salt and coarse black pepper

First make the filling. Heat the oil and briskly fry mushrooms, leeks and onion until moisture has evaporated. Stir in spinach and cottage cheese and season well with salt and pepper. Take 18 sheets of pastry and cut into squares. Using 3 sheets for each parcel, paint the top square with melted butter. Spoon a generous spoonful of mixture into the centre of each pastry square. Pull up the pastry and twist to make a parcel. I have tied them with string, which does make them more secure. Brush the outside of each parcel with melted butter, sprinkle with a little water and bake at 200 °C for 10–15 minutes or until golden brown. Serve with mixed vegetables or a fresh salad.

WINE SUGGESTION: **Unwooded Chardonnay**

COUNTRY CUISINE

Side Dishes

We grow a lot of fruit, herbs and a selection of vegetables.

There is always something different and fresh to add to the menu.

Any fruit or vegetable ripened on the tree or bush with hours of additional sunshine

just has a special flavour, intense and full, unlike anything bought in the shops.

Roast Mediterranean Vegetables

SERVES 6

A selection of vegetables such as peppers, brinjals, butternut,
pumpkin, courgettes, red onions, sweet potatoes, garlic, tomatoes
125 ml (½ cup) olive oil
125 ml (½ cup) balsamic vinegar
salt and coarse black pepper
fresh thyme or rosemary

Slice or chop the vegetables into chunks, enough for 6 servings.
Combine the olive oil and balsamic vinegar and coat the vegetables well.
Season with salt and pepper.
Place in a baking pan under the grill until the vegetables are soft and crisped on the edges.
Scattered chopped fresh thyme or rosemary over the vegetables when they are almost done.
The herbs add a lovely fragrance.

WINE SUGGESTION: Chenin Blanc

Brinjal Bake

SERVES 6

2 medium brinjals
1 medium onion
2 tomatoes
olive oil
salt and coarse black pepper
2 eggs
125 ml (½ cup) cream
125 ml (½ cup) cream cheese

Slice the brinjals, onions and tomatoes and sauté in heated olive oil until soft and lightly browned.
Spoon into a baking dish and sprinkle with salt and coarse black pepper.
Beat together the eggs, cream and cream cheese and pour over the vegetables.
Bake at 180 °C until golden brown. Serve immediately.

WINE SUGGESTION: Sauvignon Blanc

Side Dishes

Butternut in Ginger Orange Sauce

SERVES 6

butternut
butter
juice of 2 oranges
10 ml (2 tsp) grated root ginger
pinch of salt
20 ml (4 tsp) brown sugar

Peel the butternut and cut into slices. Steam or boil until just soft, then drain on a paper towel and pat dry. Brown the slices in a little butter in a frying pan, then arrange on a platter and keep warm. Stir the remaining ingredients into the pan juices. When combined and bubbling, drizzle the ginger orange sauce over the butternut slices and serve as a special vegetable dish.

Baby Green Beans and Almonds

green beans
salt
a pinch of bicarbonate of soda
slivered almonds, toasted

Trim the beans and cook in boiling water to which salt and a pinch of bicarbonate of soda have been added. Remove when still crisp (al dente) and refresh under cold running water. Serve sprinkled with a generous handful of almonds or dress the beans in your favourite dressing.

Rosemary Mash

potatoes
cream
salt
butter
fresh rosemary, finely chopped

Boil enough potatoes to make the required quantity of mash. Add cream, salt, and a generous knob of butter. Whip the rosemary into the mashed potato and serve immediately as the rosemary will start to discolour the potato.

Crispy Potato Wedges

*These are a healthy, delicious accompaniment to any hearty meat dish.
Ideal with roast lamb, venison or beef instead of roast potatoes.*

medium potatoes, scrubbed
oil
chopped fresh herbs
coarse salt

Parboil the potatoes, drain and cool. Slice into quarters and pat dry if necessary. Heat oil in a deep saucepan, drop in potato wedges and fry until crisp and brown. Sprinkle with fresh herbs and salt.

Potatoes au Gratin

SERVES 6

6 medium potatoes, peeled
salt and coarse black pepper
20 ml (4 tsp) grated onion
250 ml (1 cup) plain yoghurt
cheddar, grated
paprika

Boil potatoes until cooked through, but not too soft. Allow to cool, then cut into thick slices.
Arrange into piles consisting of 4 or 5 slices each on a baking tray and sprinkle with a little salt and pepper.
Mix together the onion and yoghurt and spoon over each pile of potato.
Top with grated cheddar cheese and a dusting of paprika and brown under the grill.

Baked Sweet Potato

SERVES 6–8

4 large or 6 medium sweet potatoes or yams, scrubbed

2 eggs

salt and coarse black pepper

250 ml (1 cup) plain yoghurt

250 ml (1 cup) cream

1 thick slice soft white bread, crumbed

grated cheddar or parmesan

Boil the sweet potatoes until cooked but still firm.
Leave the skin on and cut into thick slices and arrange in overlapping slices in a baking dish.
Beat together the eggs, salt, pepper, yoghurt, cream and breadcrumbs and pour over the potatoes.
Sprinkle with grated cheddar or parmesan cheese and bake at 180 °C for 20–30 until firm and golden brown.

Polenta and Spinach

SERVES 8

This is quite a bland side dish, so it is best served with a rich-flavoured main course. It goes particularly well with a tomato-based casserole.

375 ml (1½ cups) polenta
1.5 litres (6 cups) water
15 ml (1 Tbsp) butter
2 bunches spinach, washed and shredded
10 ml (2 tsp) salt
5 ml (1 tsp) bicarbonate of soda
olive oil

Whisk the polenta into the boiling water, reduce the heat and continue stirring until the water cooks away and the polenta thickens, about 20–30 minutes.
Stir in the butter for a rich creamy flavour.
Cook the spinach in fast-boiling water to which the salt and bicarbonate of soda has been added.
When just soft, remove and refresh in cold water.
Press the polenta into the spinach and press into a square baking tin.
Paint with olive oil and place under the grill for 10 minutes. Cut into slices or squares to serve.

Baked Tomatoes

SERVES 6-8

6-8 medium, firm, ripe tomatoes
mozzarella (optional)
fresh basil (optional)

Filling

250 ml (1 cup) precooked arborio rice
250 ml (1 cup) chopped mushrooms
15 ml (1 Tbsp) finely chopped basil
5 ml (1 tsp) chopped garlic
salt and coarse black pepper to taste
15 ml (1 Tbsp) olive oil
15 ml (1 Tbsp) lemon juice

Cut a slice off the bud end (opposite the stalk end) of each tomato and carefully scoop out the flesh.
To make the filling, combine the rice, mushrooms, basil, garlic and salt and pepper.
Drizzle with a little olive oil and lemon juice, stir to combine, then spoon into the tomato cavities.
Bake at 180 °C for 30 minutes or until tomatoes are soft.
Remove from oven and serve topped with a sliver of mozzarella and a basil leaf.

WINE SUGGESTION: **Dry Rosé**

Broccoli au Fromage

SERVES 6

45 ml (3 Tbsp) butter
125 ml (½ cup) chopped onion
500 ml (2 cups) milk
1 egg
2.5 ml (½ tsp) salt
2.5 ml (½ tsp) white pepper
40 ml (8 tsp) cornflour
125 ml (½ cup) grated cheese
1 kg fresh broccoli florets, cooked
cheese shavings
paprika

Melt the butter, add the onion and sauté until soft.
Beat together the milk, egg, salt, pepper, cornflour and the grated cheese.
Add to the onions and stir until the sauce thickens.
Pour over the broccoli, sprinkle with the cheese shavings and dust with paprika.
Brown under a preheated grill before serving.

WINE SUGGESTION: Sauvignon Blanc

Desserts

Le Petit Papillon

An old favourite loved by young and old, the crisp wings complementing the smoothness of the ice cream.

vanilla ice cream
mixed berries
melted chocolate

Caramel Wings

250 g margarine
250 g castor sugar
250 ml (1 cup) golden syrup
5 ml (1 tsp) vanilla essence
5 ml (1 tsp) lemon juice
5 ml (1 tsp) brandy
45 ml (3 Tbsp) cake flour

Melt the margarine and castor sugar, add golden syrup, vanilla, lemon juice and brandy. Lastly stir in the cake flour, mixing well. Drop spoonsful (about 20 ml [4 tsp]) of the mixture onto a baking tray, allowing room to spread. Bake at 180 °C until light brown and bubbly (they burn easily so keep an eye on them). Immediately lift with a spatula onto a cold surface and cut rounds into four. You must work quickly, but you can reheat them to soften. Each quarter is a wing. They are brittle, so take care.

Spoon a ball of rich vanilla ice cream into a bowl, decorate with two wings, berries and chocolate.

WINE SUGGESTION: Special Late Harvest

Plum Crazy

SERVES 6

*This was La Petite Ferme's first and most favourite dessert.
We grow the beautiful red Santa Rosa plums on the farm and in springtime there is
the bonus of drifts of white blossoms.*

250 ml (1 cup) water
500 ml (2 cups) sugar
12 plums, preferably Santa Rosa
250 ml (1 cup) red wine
2.5 ml (½ tsp) mixed spice

Make a syrup by combining the water and sugar and bringing them to a boil.
When boiling, add the plums and reduce the heat so that they poach very gently until soft but not mushy.
Let them cool in the syrup, then remove the plums with a slotted spoon.
Add the red wine and mixed spice to 500 ml (2 cups) of the syrup, bring to the boil and reduce slightly.
When cool, pour over the plums.
The plums are delicious served with a scoop of rich vanilla ice cream, whipped cream or thick yoghurt.
We add a meringue to complement the tartness of the plums.

WINE SUGGESTION: Merlot

Real Rich Chocolate Mousse

SERVES 16

The chocolate in this recipe is alarming but a more delicious chocolate mousse would be hard to find.

400 g milk chocolate
400 g dark chocolate
125 g soft butter
125 ml (½ cup) strong black coffee
125 ml (½ cup) brandy
1 litre (4 cups) cream
8 eggs
whipped cream and chocolate swirls to serve

Melt the chocolates, butter and coffee in the top of a double boiler.
Stir in the brandy. Beat cream until stiff and place in refrigerator.
Separate the eggs and whisk the egg whites until stiff.
Add the egg yolks to the chocolate mixture one at a time, beating well.
Finally, gently fold in the whipped cream and beaten egg whites.
Pour into a large bowl or individual glasses and refrigerate until set.
Serve topped with a swirl of cream and a chocolate decoration.

WINE SUGGESTION: Shiraz

The Ultimate Crème Brûlée

SERVES 6

*Texture is what a crème brûlée is all about – the velvety smooth custard topped with a crisp crunch is everybody's favourite. It is a versatile dessert as you can add flavourings and fruits for interest.
A few berries at the bottom come as a delicious surprise.*

5 egg yolks
25 ml (5 tsp) sugar
500 ml (2 cups) cream
2.5 ml (½ tsp) vanilla essence
castor sugar

Beat the yolks and sugar together, then stir in the cream and vanilla essence. Pour into ramekins.
Place the ramekins in a baking tin and carefully pour in hot water to reach half way up the sides of the ramekins.
Bake in a cool oven at 140 °C for about half an hour or until firm and slightly golden on top.
Remove the ramekins, cool and then refrigerate until ready to serve.
To serve, sprinkle a layer of castor sugar on top of each ramekin and place under a very hot grill until caramelised.

WINE SUGGESTION: Noble Late Harvest

Crêpe Versatility

MAKES 8–10 CREPES

125 ml (½ cup) water
125 ml (½ cup) milk
2 egg yolks
120 g cake flour

Ricotta Filling
125 ml (½ cup) raisins
15 ml (1 Tbsp) Cointreau or Van der Hum
375 g ricotta cheese
2 egg yolks
80 ml (⅓ cup) castor sugar
20 ml (4 tsp) butter
30 ml (2 Tbsp) lemon juice

Banana Filling
2–3 bananas, sliced
15 ml (1 Tbsp) butter
125 ml (½ cup) brown sugar
juice of 1 orange

Cheese and Spinach Filling
15 ml (1 Tbsp) butter
1 large bunch spinach, finely chopped
1 small onion, chopped
1 small red pepper, chopped
salt and pepper to taste
125 g blue cheese or feta, crumbled

To make the crêpes, beat together the water, milk and egg yolks, then beat in the flour. Pour enough batter into a heated pan to cover the base. When set, turn crêpe over and cook the other side. Remove and keep warm. Continue making crêpes until all the batter has been used. To make the ricotta filling, mix all the ingredients together and spoon onto the crêpes. Roll up and place in baking dish, brush with butter, then bake for 10–15 minutes at 160 °C.
To make the banana filling, fry the bananas in the butter, sugar and orange juice. When caramelized, spoon onto the crêpes, roll up and serve with cream or ice cream.
To make the cheese and spinach filling, melt the butter and sauté the spinach, onion and pepper until soft. Season with salt and pepper. Stir in the cheese. Spoon the filling onto crêpes, roll up and serve as a delicious savoury starter.

WINE SUGGESTION: Unwooded Chardonnay with savoury; Wooded Chenin Blanc with sweet

La Petite Ferme
COUNTRY CUISINE

Tarte Citron

MAKES 10–12 SLICES

This is a real classic — light and tangy.

Base
180 g cake flour
75 ml (5 Tbsp) icing sugar
75 g softened butter
pinch of salt
1 egg yolk
15 ml (1 Tbsp) water

Filling
4 eggs
125 ml (½ cup) castor sugar
200 ml (⅘ cup) fresh lemon juice
zest of 4 lemons
125 ml (½ cup) cream

whipped cream and icing sugar to serve

To make the base, put all the ingredients into a food processor and blend to make a firm dough. Place in the refrigerator for half an hour, then roll out and press into a flan tin.
Bake blind at 200 °C for 20 minutes.
To make the filling, beat the eggs and sugar until thick and pale. Add the lemon juice and zest followed by the cream.
Whip together lightly, then pour into the pastry base and bake at 180 °C for about 30 minutes until set.
Cool, then serve with whipped cream and a dusting of icing sugar.

WINE SUGGESTION: Sparkling Wine (Off-dry)

Pecan Nut Pie

MAKES 10–12 SLICES

Base
500 g cake flour
250 g soft butter
125 ml (½ cup) iced water

Filling
15 ml (1 Tbsp) brandy
5 ml (1 tsp) vanilla essence
2 eggs, well beaten
125 ml (½ cup) golden syrup
125 ml (½ cup) maple syrup
15 ml (1 Tbsp) brown sugar
500 g pecan nuts or pieces

rich vanilla ice cream or cream to serve

To make the base, sift the flour and rub in the butter. Add the water and mix quickly to make a firm dough. Press the pastry into a large fluted flan dish and place in the refrigerator while you prepare the filling. To make the filling, beat together all the ingredients except the pecan nuts. Sprinkle the nuts over the pastry base, then pour in the filling mixture. Bake at 160 °C for about 45 minutes until the pastry is golden brown and the filling set. Serve sliced with rich vanilla ice cream or cream.

WINE SUGGESTION: Noble Late Harvest

Baked Honey Pears

SERVES 6

*This is an original Huguenot recipe given to me by the Malherbe family.
We grow two varieties of pears on La Petite Ferme — Clapp's Favourite and Packham's Triumph
but I've used Beurre Boscs very successfully. Some of the new varieties are also very good.*

6 pears

250 ml (1 cup) water

125 ml (½ cup) brown sugar

125 ml (½ cup) honey

1 stick cinnamon

custard, cream or ice cream to serve

Choose pears with a good shape, but which are not too ripe.
You can peel them but we use them unpeeled (the skin is so good for you).
Make up a syrup by combining the water, sugar, honey and cinnamon and bringing to a boil.
Reduce to 375 ml (1½ cups).
If you keep the skins on, prick the pears and dip each one into the prepared syrup and transfer to a baking dish.
Bake the pears in a hot oven at 180 °C for approximately half an hour until soft and golden.
Spoon some of the reserved syrup over the pears as they bake.
Different pears require different baking times so watch them and don't let them bake for too long.
Serve with a light vanilla egg custard, cream or ice cream.

WINE SUGGESTION: Natural Sweet

Brandy Pudding

MAKES 1 LARGE PUDDING OR 12 MUFFINS

*This is such a favourite at the restaurant and a recipe
I'm always giving to people that I just had to include it.
The pudding can be made in a single bowl or in muffin tins to make individual desserts.
Brandy pudding makes a lovely alternative to Christmas pudding.
Replace the dates with raisins and add a handful of cherries.*

5 ml (1 tsp) bicarbonate of soda
250 ml (1 cup) boiling water
250 g dates, chopped
125 g butter
250 ml (1 cup) sugar
2 large eggs
250 g self-raising flour
1 ml (¼ tsp) salt
100 g pecan nuts

Syrup
20 ml (4 tsp) butter
250 ml (1 cup) sugar
150 ml (½ cup plus 5 tsp) water
125 ml (½ cup) brandy

whipped cream or ice cream to serve

Dissolve the bicarb in the boiling water, pour over the dates, stir and leave to cool. Beat the butter and sugar until fluffy, then add the eggs, beating well. Stir in the flour, salt, dates and pecan nuts. When well combined, spoon into a greased bowl or muffin tins and bake at 180 °C for 30–40 minutes until cooked through. Meanwhile make the syrup by simmering the butter, sugar and water for 5 minutes, then stir in the brandy. Pour the syrup over the pudding or muffins as they come out of the oven. You can prick it to allow every drop to soak in. Serve warm with whipped cream or ice cream.

WINE SUGGESTION: Port

Real Farm Apple Tart

MAKES 1 TART

*Nothing measures up to fresh Granny Smith apples.
You can use tinned pie apples but for an extra special tart use the fresh ones.*

8–10 apples
125 ml (½ cup) water
sugar or honey to taste
5 ml (1 tsp) cornflour
brown sugar

Pastry
250 g butter or margarine
250 ml (1 cup) castor sugar
2 eggs, lightly beaten
500 g self-raising flour, sifted

whipped cream to serve

First make the pastry base.
Cream the butter and castor sugar, then stir in the eggs and flour. Press half the dough into a deep pie dish, reserving the rest for the topping. Place in the refrigerator to firm up.
Peel the apples and cut into chunks.
Place in a saucepan with the water and gently poach until just soft.
Sweeten with sugar or honey and thicken with the cornflour mixed with a little water.
Cool, then spoon onto the pastry base.
Grate the remaining dough on top of the apple and sprinkle with brown sugar.
Bake at 180 °C for about 40 minutes or until nicely browned.
Delicious served with whipped cream.

WINE SUGGESTION: Sweet-styled Chenin Blanc

Pavlova

MAKES/SERVES 8–10

*This old classic is still a favourite because it's so versatile.
You can make up a batch of meringue nests and keep them in a sealed container for several weeks.
They are delicious with sliced tropical fruit, peach slices or the delicious berries which are in season for several months of the year. Invest in a piping bag and nozzle, although you can spoon the mixture onto a baking sheet.*

Meringue Mixture
4 egg whites
250 g castor sugar

Topping
whipped cream
sliced mixed fruit or berries

Coulis
250 ml (1 cup) sugar
250 ml (1 cup) berries
125 ml (½ cup) water

Beat the egg whites for 2 minutes then slowly add half the sugar and beat for a further 4 minutes until very stiff.
Add the remaining sugar all together and fold in carefully – don't stir. Pipe or spoon the mixture onto a baking sheet and place in a preheated oven at 140 °C for 1 hour, then switch off the oven and leave the meringue in the oven overnight.
A thermofan oven works best but alternatively place the baking sheet on the top shelf of the oven so that the meringues don't burn underneath.
Top with whipped cream and sliced fruit or berries. As an extra special touch drizzle some colourful berry coulis over the top or on the plate.
To make the coulis, bring the sugar, berries and water to a boil, then purée.

WINE SUGGESTION: **Special Late Harvest**

Flavoured Butters

These are always useful if you are having a buffet or a cheese and wine party. They just add a touch of pizzaz to ordinary French loaves, biscuits or other breads. We have four favourites:

500 g butter

Anchovy Butter
7 ml (1 heaped tsp) finely chopped anchovies or anchovy paste

Herb Butter
7 ml (1 heaped tsp) finely chopped mixed fresh herbs
½ clove garlic, chopped

Mustard Butter
7 ml (1 heaped tsp) Dijon mustard
2.5 ml (½ tsp) mustard seeds

Chilli Butter
7 ml (1 heaped tsp) finely chopped red chilli (not the seeds or veins) or
5 ml (1 tsp) sweet red pepper
a few drops Tabasco sauce

Remove the butter from the refrigerator and allow to stand overnight.
Divide the butter into four and beat the flavourings into each quarter.
Pot the butters and return them to the refrigerator to firm up.

Country Loaf

MAKES 1 LARGE OR 2 SMALL LOAVES

This is a real farm loaf not only in flavour, but in size - it fills a large loaf tin.
You might prefer to make two smaller loaves or for a change use a deep round cake tin.

375 ml (1½ cups) cake flour
375 ml (1½ cups) Nutty Wheat flour
180 ml (¾ cup) oats
180 ml (¾ cup) digestive bran
180 ml (¾ cup) sunflower seeds
1 pkt instant yeast
375 ml (1½ cups) lukewarm water
125 ml (½ cup) oil
125 ml (½ cup) honey, molasses or golden syrup

Mix together the flours, oats, bran and sunflower seeds. Mix together the yeast, water, oil and honey and stir into the dry ingredients, mixing well.
The mixture should be firm but moist. Add a little more water if you feel it's too dry.
Spoon into a greased loaf tin or tins and bake in a preheated oven at 180 °C for 1 hour, or until a skewer inserted in the centre comes out clean.
For a loaf with a difference, add a handful of raisins or chopped dried apricots.

La Petite Ferme
COUNTRY CUISINE

Fish Stock

MAKES 2.5 LITRES (10 CUPS)

Fish stock is flavoured by the fish used and must never be cooked for too long, or it will become bitter.

2 kg fish bones and trimmings
1 large onion
2 large carrots
1 stick celery
250 ml (1 cup) dry white wine
about 12 peppercorns
2 bay leaves
juice of a lemon
2.5 litres (10 cups) water

Combine all the ingredients and bring to a boil.
Skim the surface, reduce the heat and simmer gently for about 20 minutes,
then strain through a fine sieve.

Glühwein

MAKES 1 LITRE (4 CUPS)

We serve this when there is snow on the mountain tops and a really warming drink is needed.

750 ml (1 bottle) red wine
250 ml (1 cup) orange juice
250 ml (1 cup) water
1 stick cinnamon
12 whole cloves
30 ml (2 Tbsp) brown sugar
orange slices studded with cloves to serve

Place all the ingredients, except the orange slices, in a saucepan and heat gently. Strain and serve hot with half a slice of orange studded with cloves in each glass. More sugar can be added if you prefer a sweeter drink.

Non-Alcoholic Celebration Punch

MAKES 5 LITRES (20 CUPS)

This is ideal as a thirst quencher at weddings or any celebration on a hot summer's day.

10 rooibos tea bags
1 litre (4 cups) boiling water
375 ml (1½ cups) granadilla juice
375 ml (1½ cups) lime juice
2 litres (8 cups) soda water
1 litre (4 cups) lemonade
apples, pears, firm peaches, pineapples, nectarines and plums, chopped
500 ml (2 cups) sugar
ice and sprigs of mint to serve

Drop the tea bags into the boiling water and allow to infuse.
When cool, strain the tea and add the granadilla and lime juices, the soda water and lemonade.
Lastly, add the fruit and the sugar to taste.
Stir together well. Before serving, add 3–4 trays of ice.
The punch must be well chilled. Spoon a little fruit into each champagne glass,
top up with punch and garnish with a sprig of mint.

Miscellaneous

Apple or Crab Apple Jelly

*If you are lucky enough to have a crab apple tree,
this delicious jelly is the very best to serve with venison, turkey, quail or a game meatloaf.
Granny Smith apples can also be used, but the jelly is pale in colour.
The apples must be fresh otherwise they lack the necessary pectin to set the jelly.
My grandmother taught me to make jams, jellies and marmalades,
and to bottle the Santa Rosa plums we use in our desserts.*

crab apples or apples

sugar

Place the crab apples (whole) or roughly chopped apples into a large saucepan and just cover with water.
Boil for about 1 hour until soft and mushy.
Tie a piece of cloth (I use an old tablecloth) over a bucket, leaving a sag in the middle.
Pour the pulp into the cloth and allow it to drip through overnight.
DO NOT press or stir. Remove the cloth and pulp and you are left with a clear liquid in the bucket.
Measure the liquid into a large saucepan and add an equal quantity of sugar, e.g. to 1 litre (4 cups) of juice add 1 litre (4 cups) of sugar. Boil rapidly, stirring only until the sugar has dissolved. Skim off any scum that forms.
After about 30 minutes, a few drops of the mixture should set when placed on a cold saucer and allowed to cool.
If not, boil for a little while longer.
In the meantime, wash and sterilize some bottles by placing them in a hot oven.
Pour in the syrup and seal. The syrup should be firm and jellied when cool.

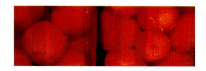

Index

Anchovy butter 121
Apple jelly 126
Apple soup, curried 20
Apple tart, real farm 117

Banana filling (crêpes) 108
Beef, medallions of, and oyster mushrooms 77
Blue cheese dressing 53
Bobotie 73
Brandy pudding 116
Brinjal bake 88
Broccoli au fromage 98
Butter
  Anchovy 121
  Chilli 121
  Herb 121
  Mustard 121
Butternut in ginger orange sauce 91

Calamari Mediterranean style 61
Carrot and ginger soup 22
Cheese and spinach filling (crêpes) 108
Chicken
  and almond salad 42
  liver pâté 37
  roulade with light curry sauce 64
  Stuffed baby chickens 62

Thai chilli chicken breasts 67
Chicken roulade with light curry sauce 64
Chilli butter 121
Chilli sauce 67
Chive sauce 46
Chocolate mousse, real rich 105
Country loaf 122
Crab apple jelly 126
Crème brûlée, the ultimate 106
Crêpe fillings
  Banana 108
  Cheese and spinach 108
  Ricotta 108
Crêpe versatility 108
Cucumber soup, chilled 26
Curry sauce, light 64

Desserts
  Baked honey pears 114
  Brandy pudding 116
  Crêpe versatility 108
  Le Petit papillon 101
  Pavlova 118
  Pecan nut pie 113
  Plum crazy 102
  Real farm apple tart 117
  Real rich chocolate mousse 105

Tarte citron 110
The ultimate crème brûlée 106
Dill sauce 49
Duck, panfried, and plum sauce 68

Fennel yoghurt sauce 38
Fish
  Calamari Mediterranean style 61
  Crumbed mussels 41
  Fish fillets with two toppings 57
  Fish pot (soup) 33
  Malay pickled fish 50
  Salmon trout mousse with fennel yoghurt sauce 38
  Salmon trout parcels 58
  Smoked salmon and blinis 46
  Stock 123
  Trout bisque 28
  Trout terrine 49
Fish pot (soup) 33

Glüwein 124
Grain salad, hot 44
Green beans (baby) and almonds 91
Guacamole with spicy chilli salsa 45

Herb butter 21
Hollandaise sauce 58

Kudu casserole 83
Kudu (smoked) salad 53

Lamb, Greek, with minted yoghurt 74
Le Petit papillon 101
Liver and bacon 79

Malay pickled fish 50
Meat
  Bobotie 73
  Greek lamb and minted yoghurt 74
  Kudu casserole 83
  Liver and bacon 79
  Medallions of beef and oyster mushrooms 77
  Pork medallions and prunes 70
  Venison with red wine sauce 80
Mediterranean soup, chunky 19
Mediterranean topping with sun-dried tomatoes (for fish) 57
Mediterranean vegetables, roast 87
Melba toast 37
Minted yoghurt sauce 74

Mousse, real rich
    chocolate 105
Mousse, salmon trout
    with fennel yoghurt
    sauce 38
Mulligatawny soup 27
Mushrooms en croûte 40
Mussels, crumbed 41
Mustard butter 121
Mustard topping
    (for fish) 57

Onion and herb soup,
    rich 34
Oyster mushroom sauce 75

Pavlova 118
Pear and blue cheese
    soup 24
Pears, baked honey
    pears 114
Pecan nut pie 113
Pickled fish, Malay 50
Plum crazy 102
Plum sauce 68
Polenta and spinach 95
Pork medallions and
    prunes 70
Potato
    and spring onion soup 30
    rosemary mash 92
    wedges, crispy 92
Potatoes au gratin 93
Prune sauce 70

Punch, non-alcoholic
    celebration punch 125

Red wine sauce 82
Ricotta filling (crêpes) 108
Rosemary mash 92
Roulade, chicken, with
    light curry sauce 64

Salads
    Chicken and almond
        salad 42
    Hot grain salad 44
    Smoked kudu salad
        with blue cheese
        dressing 53
    Spinach and bacon
        salad 54
Salmon trout mousse
    with fennel yoghurt
    sauce 38
Salmon trout parcels 58
Sauces
    Chilli sauce
    Chive 46
    Dill 49
    Fennel yoghurt 38
    Hollandaise 58
    Light curry 64
    Minted yoghurt 74
    Oyster mushroom 77
    Plum 68
    Prune 70
    Red wine 80

Smoked kudu salad
    with blue cheese
    dressing 53
Smoked salmon and
    blinis 46
Soups
    Carrot and ginger 22
    Chilled cucumber 26
    Chunky Mediterranean 19
    Curried apple 20
    Fish pot 33
    Mulligatawny 27
    Pear and blue cheese 24
    Potato and spring
        onion 30
    Rich onion and herb 34
    Spinach and feta 23
    Split pea and Eisbein 31
    Trout bisque 28
Spinach
    and bacon salad 54
    and feta soup 23
Split pea and Eisbein
    soup 31
Starters
    Chicken liver pâté 37
    Crumbed mussels 41
    Guacamole with spicy
        chilli salsa 45
    Malay pickled fish 50
    Mushrooms en croûte 40
    Smoked salmon and
        blinis 46
    Trout terrine 49

Stock, fish 123
Sweet potato, baked 94

Tarte citron 110
Thai chilli chicken
    breasts 67
Tomatoes, baked 97
Trout bisque 28
Trout terrine 49

Vegetable dishes
    Baby green beans and
        almonds 91
    Baked sweet potato 94
    Baked tomatoes 97
    Brinjal bake 88
    Broccoli au fromage 98
    Butternut in ginger
        orange sauce 91
    Crispy potato wedges 92
    Polenta and spinach 95
    Potatoes au gratin 93
    Roast Mediterranean
        vegetables 87
    Rosemary mash 92
    Vegetarian parcel 84
    Venison with red wine
        sauce 80

Wine sauce, red 80